POLAR

INERTIA

Published by

Los Angeles Forum for Architecture and Urban Design

PO Box 291774, Los Angeles CA 90029-8774

Book Design by Henri Lucas + Davey Whitcraft

for WILLEM AUGUSTUS, 2007

Typeface Lux Sans designed by Greg Lindy

Intro by Greg Goldin, Text by Ted Kane and Rick Miller,

Photographs by Ted Kane

This project is sponsored in part by a grant from the
City of Los Angeles Department of Cultural Affairs.

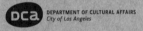 DEPARTMENT OF CULTURAL AFFAIRS
City of Los Angeles

Published in the United States of America

ISBN # 978-0-9763166-3-3

Cataloging-in-Publication data for this book is available from

the Library of Congress

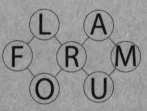

los angeles **forum** for architecture and urban design

NATIONAL
ENDOWMENT
FOR THE ARTS
A great nation
deserves great art.

Distributed by r.a.m. publications + distributions, inc.

2525 Michigan Avenue, Bldg. #A2

Santa Monica, CA 90404

For more information on other publications and programs of

the Los Angeles Forum for Architecture and Urban Design,

please visit their website at www.laforum.org

This project was made possible by the support and funding

of the Los Angeles Forum for Architecture and Urban Design,

the City of Los Angeles Department of Cultural Affairs,the

National Endowment for the Arts and the Graham Foundation for

Advanced Studies in the Fine Arts.

RESEARCH AND PHOTOGRAPHS BY TED KANE

POLAR
INERTIA

Migrating Urban Systems

CONTENTS:

Credits   p. 2

Introduction by Greg Goldin   p. 5

ESSAYS

1. **Migrating Cities**
    Adaptable Mobile Communities   p. 6

2. **Private Urban Infrastructures of Los Angeles:**
    The Rise of Competing and Redundant Urban Networks   p. 14

3. **Taco Trucks:**
    Emergent Urbanism in Los Angeles   p. 24

    Bibliography   p. 31

    Acknowledgements   p. 32

IMAGES

a. **RVs: Urban Camping**   p. 34

b. **RVs: Border Camping**   p. 46

c. **Camouflaged Cell Phone Towers**   p. 58

d. **Los Angeles Taco Trucks**   p. 70

INTRODUCTION

Polar inertia is a term coined by Paul Virilio to describe the tendency of technology to rapidly bring about an instantaneous present, replacing the distance of space and the sovereignty of territory into a single pole of inertia. Ted Kane has adopted this metaphor for his study of the sweeping changes that mobility and networked communications are making in cities today. At the edges and limits of technology and geography, this single pole is silently and imperceptibly exerting itself.

Los Angeles, to no one's surprise, is yet again the laboratory. As Reyner Banham once observed that in Los Angeles "mobility outweighs monumentality." What was true for the automobile is fast becoming true for the home. It is possible today to live on wheels, to be completely transient and yet remain completely connected. The traditional fixtures of a household – the kitchen and bathroom – and the typical links to the outside – the telephone and television – are no longer stationary. Thousands upon thousands of Americans live, with no specific geographic boundaries, in RVs. Out in the wastelands of the Sonoran Desert, armadas of gas-guzzling homes-on-wheels congregate and winter, like snowbirds, on barren government land or abandoned Wal-Mart parking lots. In Los Angeles fleets of Taco Trucks fan out daily, delivering meals along the unseen and unknown byways, at jobsites and factories. They follow an unchartable path, laid out by cell phones and instinct, extending and receding cultural way stations that do not appear on any map.

These are but two examples of the changing ebb and flow of the city. Each day, a recombinant magic is conjured by the intersection of low-tech internal combustion and high-tech microwave. Geography begins to lose its meaning. Hooked up – and hooked on – a network, many people travel through the city and haven't an idea that it is there. Where, exactly, is the city when its residents can, for all practical purposes, be at two places at once – here and there, neither and both?

Amid such fluidity, it becomes increasingly difficult to decipher what constitutes a city. In the provocative pages that follow, Ted Kane looks at "Urban Car Camping," "Boondocking," food catering trucks, cellular and wireless networks, to tease out where city life predicated on total mobility may be headed. Among other things, while cities are becoming more cosmopolitan, they are also becoming more thoroughly dependent. He argues that the corporate-controlled wireless world is expanding the meaning of urbanity while constricting the bedrock virtue of citizenship. The new citizen is at once free to roam and yet at the mercy of powerful corporate interests capable of compressing all political discussion into the demands of the marketplace. As Kane notes, "as we gain insight into this meshwork of overlapping infrastructures, we open new ways of understanding the city." –GREG GOLDIN

TED KANE

MIGRATI

ADAPTABLE MOBILE COMMUNITIES

URBA

(1)

C

"We have entered another kind of capital which corresponds to another kind of population. We no longer populate stationariness (cities as great parking lots for populations), we populate the time changing place, travel time" –PAUL VIRILIO

BORDER

Migrating Cities

The thousands of Recreational Vehicles camped on the streets of Los Angeles each evening, and the communities of over a million mobile inhabitants camped along the US/Mexico border each winter are evidence of fault lines beginning to separate urban form from its geographic roots. The Recreational Vehicle Industry Association estimates that there are over 8.8 million RVs currently on the road, and among these it is estimated that more than 1.5 million people are living full-time in their vehicles.[1] Living independently in their trailers, these citizens have redefined the idea of communities and challenged our reading of cities as fixed settlements. The migrating city is composed of a fluid pattern made possible by the expanding infrastructures that facilitate the autonomy of the individual. Architects and planners have largely neglected an analysis of these mobile communities, exposing the fixation that currently binds urban planning to issues of property development. The shift towards an increasingly mobile population is a precursor of larger trend in contemporary culture, and forecasts a near future in which mobility will be central to the debate about how our cities are defined, governed and regulated.

In Las Vegas, Phoenix and other fast-growing western American cities, the number of RV parks has exploded over the last decade.[2] This upsurge resulted not only from the growing numbers of baby boomer retirees but also to meet a demand by telecommunication contract laborers, construction workers, and seasonal laborers, all attracted to the daily rent agreements common at RV parks. These new migratory proletarians are laborers who need to follow unpredictable workflows that can take them to different cities throughout the year.[3] A parking space, propane connection, satellite TV, WiFi Internet connection and sewer hookup all create plug-in communities and an adaptable alternative

to the traditional suburban grid. Today 35-to-54 year olds own more RVs than any other age group, with 1 in 10 vehicle owning households also owning an RV.[4] The adoption of the RV is a natural evolution for this population who grew up amidst the increased mobility that occurred following WWII, with the build out of the federal highway system connecting the country[5] Migratory patterns that rooted early in life have increased a desire for flexibility and autonomy throughout life.[6] The RV has come to symbolize a freedom of living, providing the ability to be home without having to be fixed to a particular place.

The full time mobile resident population is composed of a diverse mix of demographics, representing the entire spectrum of income and cultural background. The full-time RV resident population includes retirees, seasonal workers, contract laborers, the mobile homeless, freelance workers, thrifty and independently wealthy, each of whom has chosen mobility for a combination of economic, convenience, social, medical, or recreational considerations. A large portion of these full-time campers are Boondocking, a term used to describe a particular brand of independent camping that is done without the benefit of "hookups" or amenities common to RV parks. These RV-ers live on public lands, Wal-Mart parking lots, truck stops, or city streets – anywhere that lacks fixed services. While the RV park is a close relative of the suburban development, the growth of Boondocking has splintered our idea of community into a flexible entity that could reconvene anywhere. The two most visible forms of Boondocking, the phenomena of Street Camping and Border Camping, each provide insight into the factors influencing the development of the migrating city: a city that isn't planned but is rather the result of a fluid pattern of living that emerges within a flexible network.

Urban Street Camping

The reality is that for many, living full-time in an RV is less a convenience, and more a necessity as the cost of housing in Los Angeles has far outpaced income.[7] The mobile homeless, as they are often called are the perennially underemployed, disabled, or unemployed who find camping on the city streets in an RV to be the best option available. Deftly penetrating the everyday streets of the city, thousands of residents are now living full-time in older generation RVs clustered along the main arterial roads of Los Angeles, making it one of the first cities to have to grapple with the desire of some of its residents to live on the streets full-time.[8] In Los Angeles, parking on most streets is free, but a vehicle must be moved every 72 hours, as well as during street cleanings. The attention needed to move an RV, maintain it and fill up the gas means that majority of mobile homeless are not mentally ill or drug addicted as you might find among the general homeless population, but are typically working adults aged 35-55, some with school age children. The mobile homeless typically have some income either through recycling, low wage work, or through disability or veterans benefits, but not enough to afford an apartment. The streets offer few comforts, but the RV retains the safety and privacy of an individual dwelling, a better choice than the lack of privacy of homeless shelters and single room occupancy hotels.

The density of mobile campers is most visible in the coastal communities of West Los Angeles, which ironically also boast some of the most expensive real estate in the United States. What draws the RVs here is a combination of factors including the availability of beach showers and bathrooms, several homeless food kitchens, and the abundance of recyclable plastics and aluminum that beach goers and businesses leave behind. The influx of campers is pitting the permanent coastal residents, who worry about the possible effects on property values and the impact on limited parking, against the mobile residents. Beach real estate has priced out most people from living in the vicinity of the beach, yet an RV can still park alongside multi-million dollar homes in Venice and take advantage of the cleaner ocean air.

Cities have begun to clamp down on the campers, as Santa Monica recently did by implementing neighborhood parking districts, making it illegal for non-residents to park in residential neighborhoods, which pushed the campers further south to Venice which doesn't have permit parking. Venice has countered with new restrictions on the heights of parked vehicles in a clear attempt to restrict RVs on certain streets. The conflicts between angry homeowners and campers can escalate into verbal abuse, threats and slashed tires , which has pushed most of the RVs toward commercial streets or areas near storage yards or industrial buildings, where they are less likely to be hassled. The street campers often form a community by clustering in groups, such as along Rose Avenue in Venice where as many as 8 RVs often park back to back, allowing them to keep an eye on each other in a potentially hostile environment. These groups also commonly share gas-powered electric generators, and will help each other push an RV that is having difficulty moving for its required pilgrimage to a new location every 72 hours. The street campers have created a collaborative form of community that has its own culture and autonomy, yet is in constant flux geographically.

These mobile citizens are living outside the current real estate driven form of governance, where the rights and privileges of citizens to vote, attend school and pay taxes are closely tied to having a permanent address. The RV has abandoned real estate and adopted the street as a social and public space, a concept of the street that was largely abandoned with

G CITIES

N STREET

MPING +

AMPING

the advent of the single-family subdivision from which Los Angeles formed. The streets of Los Angeles were primarily designed for efficient movement, so their re-appropriation for living is an exceptional notion. As the popularity of RV living increases, and a larger segment of society begins living exclusively on the streets, the concept of the street as a public space will come under increasing pressure, as will the debate about how to incorporate this new mobile class in our concept of communities.

Border Camping

The American Southwest has become the point of congregation for Boondockers living "off the grid." Attracted by the warm weather and cheap camping, the population explodes every winter with an influx of seasonal residents, all of whom find they can stretch a fixed income further here than anywhere else in the country. Aiding the influx is the proximity to the Mexican border where medical prescriptions, clothing, liquor, and dental service are available at reduced rates.

The increasing sophistication of Recreation Vehicles has made raw camping a viable option, even for the less adventurous. Many RVs now have self-contained water, sewage storage, solar panels, air conditioning, electric generators, satellite tv and internet, allowing them to function completely off the grid, with only occasional treks for refilling the water tank, buying food, and emptying the sewage tank.[9] RVs are increasing in size and sophistication, taking on more of the feel of fixed homes, aided by the fact that interest on RV mortgages can now be deducted from federal taxes.[10] It is now possible to remain connected even when miles from the nearest town or power line.

Raw camping is most common on Bureau of Land Management (BLM) lands, and in government established wilderness areas, called Long Term Visitor Areas (LTVA), where for around one dollar a day campers can purchase a visitors permit and camp for 14 days in a 28-day period. (After the 14th day of occupation campers must move outside of a 25-mile radius of the previous location in order to minimize damage to a single area).[11] There are no hook-ups or electricity in the parks, but there is generally a water outlet and sewer and trash disposal located at various points. Outside LTVA designated areas, Boondockers can camp for free on BLM desert land where no services are offered. In the winter months, the small town of Quartzite in western Arizona, which is surrounded by BLM and LTVA visitor areas, has recorded over a million RV visitors for its Gem show, blossoming from 2500 residents in the summer into the second largest city in Arizona, after Phoenix.[12] These mass migrations have been increasing yearly, with word of mouth spreading to the north in summer and bringing larger flocks of converts back to the southern border each winter.[13] But this city is without industry, and minimal services; it is a strangely primitive society, but as Jean Baudrillard once said of Los Angeles, it is a primitive society of the future.

Camping in the raw desert attracts both the expected outcasts and eccentrics, along with the affluent who seem to relish the autonomy of independent living. In the desert wilderness parks you can often find 20+ year old dilapidated RVs living in proximity to state of the art RVs valued at nearly a million dollars. The economic status associated by zip code is absent in the open desert, yet cultural differences are still clearly visible in the way the RVs choose to cluster and create ad hock communities. The retirees and recreation campers are the most social, often parking in tight groupings of 4 or more RVs, while the less maintained RVs tend to be solitary campers parked a safe distance from any others with a clear view in all directions. An example is Slab City, a free

camping site on a former marine base in the Mojave desert
of California, where a self-segregating pattern has developed
among RV campers who settle into two groups: retirees living
in newer RVs, parked close together, and tending to stay only
for the winter; and older RVs, vans and late model buses,
who reside year-around, deeper into the less accessible,
more private areas of the park. Although the two groups
share this abandoned base, they remain culturally separate
and mildly suspicious of each other. Even within this de-
located space, residents find a way to establish temporary
connections and communities based on shared interests or
perceived common values.

The migrating city is the genesis of a city taken over by
the extremes of individualism—a place made possible by
the redundant infrastructures that facilitate the increasing
autonomy of the individual. Yet, at this extreme edge, mobility
is pushed outside the boundaries of legal protections,
where voting rights and access to schools and government
services are increasingly controlled by the demonstration
of a permanent address. For many full-time RVers their only
address is a post office box and a mail-forwarding center
perhaps thousands of miles away. These migrating citizens
operate outside of normal jurisdictions, creating a situation
in which they are subject to the authority imposed by federal,
state and local laws, and yet, as non-residents, unable to
benefit from the protections of these same laws. As cities
continue to unmoor from the anchors of fixed residency and
float within a zone of global communication, commerce and
infrastructure, the rules now governing democracy and cities
will also need to be widened, further blurring the established
boundaries of political territory.

REFERENCES:

– Baudrillard, Jean. *America*. Verso Press, 1988.

– Gumble, Andrew. "Quartzsite." *The Independent* - London. April 10, 1999.

– Fulton, William. *The Reluctant Metropolis: The politics of Urban Growth in Los Angeles*. Solano Press Books, 1997.

– Kelly, Kevin. *Out of Control: The New Biology of Machines, Social Systems, and the Economic World*. Perseus Books, 1994.

– Los Angeles Homeless Services Authority, 2005 *Greater Los Angeles Homeless Count*. Los Angeles Homeless Services Authority, 2005.

– Leduff, Charlie. "*Parked in a desert, Waiting Out the Winter of Life*." New York Times, December 17, 2004.

– Nieves, Evelyn. "*Slab City Journal; for thousands, a town of concrete slabs is a winter retreat*." New York Times, February 18, 2001.

– Palmer, Susan, "Concrete Wilderness, RV travelers find parking-lot camping is convenient- and free" *The Registar-Guard Eugene Or*. August 21, 2005.

– Smith, Linell. "In RVs, older Americans going mobile" *Baltimore Sun*, May 27, 2007.

– Urbana Ian. "Keeping it secret as the family car becomes a home." *New York Times*, April 2, 2006.

– Varnelis, Kazys and Sumrell, Robert. *Blue Monday: Stories of Absurd Realities and Natural Philosophies*. Actar Press, 2007.

– Virilio, Paul. *Lost Dimension*. Semiotext(e) 1991.

– Wallis Allan D. *Wheel Estate. The Rise and Decline of Mobile Homes*. The Johns Hopkins University Press, 1991.

– Wolinsky, Cary. "America's Largest Parking Lot (Quartzsite, Arizona)." *National Geographic*, January 1, 2001.

NOTES:

[1] According to industry statistics compile by the Recreation Vehicle Industry Association (RVIA). There are 8.8 million RVs on the road, this is a 58% increase since 1980.

[2] It has been estimated that approximately 75,000 people live in Phoenix area RV parks and National Statistics show, according to a survey conducted by Yesawich, Pepperdine, Brown, and Russell (YPBR) for the National Association of RV Parks and Campgrounds (ARVC)., that there are over 16,000 RV parks in the United states and approximately 8500 privately owned parks. With an average of 133 spaces, there is enough parking spaces for 2.12 million RVs, nearly double the numbers of 20 years ago.

[3] The term "Workampers" has been used to describe these full time RV'ers who are not retired and travel in their RVs to job opportunities throughout the country.
The website http://www.workamper.com provides job listing and advise for this community.

[4] Figures based on industry statistics compiled by the Recreation Vehicle Industry Association (RVIA), the fulltime
population is estimated to be around 15% of RV owners.
http://www.rvia.org/AM/Template.cfm?Section=
RV_Ownership_Trends

[5] In 1956 Dwight Eisenhower signed the Federal Highway Act,
enabling the construction of a national wide system of freeways connecting American urban centers.

[6] Arizona State researcher Kevin McHugh has been document-
ing the snowbird migratory phenomena which now doubles
the size of Yuma Arizona each winter. He finds that the
increased mobility of babyboomers which occurred because
of jobs shifting away from industrial states created a need
for many boomers to uproot from their hometowns for
economic opportunities. This mobility has continued in their
retirement, a pattern of cyclical migration between multiple
locations has become a key part of their identity.

[7] As Ian Urbina mentioned in her article on the mobile homeless, a survey conducted by the National Low Income Housing
Coalition found that a full time worker on minium wage
couldn't afford a one-bedroom apartment anywhere in the
country at average market rates.

[8] According to a survey of overall homeless in Los Angeles
County which found there are 88,000 homeless in LA County
and of those it was reported 9.8% reported living in a RV or
Car, which is approximately 8600 residents.

[9] As Steve Dougherty a travel writer for the New York Times
said "An RV has more living space than my last Manhattan

apartment... tricked out with a satellite dish on the roof,
flat-screen TVs, computer hookups and a surround-sound
component stereo system that puts my own modest home
system to shame."

[10] Consult your tax advisor.

[11] The Bureau of Land Management is a government organization within the US Department of the Interior responsible for
managing approximately 268 million acres of Federally owned
lands, mostly located in the southwestern united states or
Alaska. The Long Term Visitor Areas (LTVA) were established
to accommodate the increasing demand for long-term
seasonal visitation, they are open only during the winter
season from March through November.

[12] For a fascinating look at the emergent properties of Quartzsite see AUDC's essay Swarm Intelligence: Quartzsite,
Arizona.(Varnelis/Sumrell).

[13] As chronicled by Cary Wolinskyi in a Nationa Geographic
article on Quartzsite entitled "America's Largest Parking Lot,
Quartzsite Arizona" January 2007.

TED KANE + RICK MILLER

PRIVATE INFRAST OF LOS ANG

②

THE RISE OF COMPETING
+ REDUNDANT URBAN NETWORKS

"The contemporary urban environment is composed and recomposed by each individual everyday around literal and virtual itineraries, and not in relation to a fixed arrangement of places. The city is tied together, not by space and built form, but by this itinerary executed through space in real time."

—ALBERT POPE[1]

A new stratum of infrastructure is settling over Los Angeles. Unlike previous developments, this new infrastructure isn't planned by publicly directed municipal entities but rather by privately operated and competing corporations. Lacking the heroic visibility of past civil works (from Mulholland-era hydrology to Eisenhower-era freeways), these new systems are projected along the airwaves or in fiber optic cables, in realms all but invisible to the average citizen. Even their sole outposts in the material world, cellular phone towers, are receding from view, camouflaged as palm trees or church steeples that blend into their suburban surroundings. But the disguises need not be so clever, as the visual background noise of the city already effectively hides towers in plain sight.[2] Belying their invisibility, these new networks of communication have as much impact on the development of the city as the freeways before them. The rise of privately funded infrastructure and the subsequent decline of public control represent a new corporate model of urban planning, with implications for the future development of the city. We must begin by examining the organization and methodology of these new networks in order to discover the processes by which they shape our world.

Regional Patterns

As a dispersed, multi-centric city Los Angeles has relied on, and has been committed to infrastructure for much of its history. Freeways, aqueducts, and dams are not only critical to the city's smooth operation, but were essential to its very existence and its growth into a city of over 12 million inhabitants.[3] These enormous undertakings have become emblematic of the collective urban psyche. Historically, infrastructural developments were integrated into the city's growth, linking the urban needs of both private and public constituencies —including Cold War defense logistics at the federal scale, localized real estate interests of the likes of Colis and Henry Huntington and the Chandler family, and the very real need for commercial links between disparate communities. [4] The freeway system elevated transportation to a public network of regional proportions, its gestation a result of federal, state, and regional interests acting together allowing a regional city to form around a new trajectory of movement removed from the ubiquitous homogeneity of the urban grid. [5] Los Angeles's residents quickly adopted the car and celebrated the freeway for its ability to connect the larger political entity of the city while maintaining the autonomy of the individual. The freeway imposed a different sense of place, one where each driver is made into the center of his or her own universe. As Reyner Banham observed,

> "A domestic or sociable journey in Los Angeles does
> not end so much at the door of one's destination as at
> the off-ramp of the freeway... in part this is a comment
> on the shear vastness of the movement pattern of
> Los Angeles, but more than that it is an acknowledge-
> ment that the freeway system in its totality is now
> a single comprehensible place, a coherent state of
> mind, a complete way of life" [6]

The popularity of the regional transportation system not only helped connect the dispersed city but also acted to weaken any attempts at a cohesive regional plan, as the freeway fueled a further dispersal of the city into a patchwork of cities each seeking greater autonomy. The regional city became a city of multiple overlapping jurisdictions—a legal quagmire—as Gerald Frug has described the phenomena, where "residents of metropolitan areas live in a multitude of legally defined jurisdictions with different borders: the areas defined by school districts, transportation districts, redevelopment authorities, park districts and the like often differ not only from city borders but from each other." [7]

Cellular Network

It is within this vacuum of myopic jurisdictions that the private infrastructure now flourishes, taking advantage of the gaps in oversight to create new, private realms unburdened by the equal access that is the obligation of a public entity.

Like the freeways before them, wireless networks hold out the promise to spatially liberate the citizen by connecting the city without undermining the autonomy of the individual citizen. The wireless network spans the extensive geographic breadth of the city creating new connections where the free-way left off. However, this new infrastructure is no longer a part of a regional plan; rather it is being carved out by private corporations competing for market share. These are commer-cial enterprises, which by their very nature are competitive yet redundant. Today in Los Angeles five telecommunications corporations—Verizon, Sprint/NexTel, T-Mobile, and AT&T are operating simultaneously, stitching together independent wireless phone networks based on their own strategic models.

Though these companies are publicly held entities in terms of their capital raised via stocks, their operations and networks are shielded from public view, making it difficult for municipal authorities to influence their formation and trajectory. Opening further fissures, local jurisdictional oversight was limited by the Telecommunications Act of 1996, which pre-vented states and local governments from "regulating the placement, construction, and modification of personal wire-less service facilities on the basis of the environmental effects of radio frequency emissions to the extent that such facilities comply with the Commission's [FCC's] regulations concerning such emissions." [8] As interpreted by the cell phone companies and defended by the Federal Communications Commission, this law has effectively eliminated the ability of local govern-

RBAN

UCTURES

LES

Private Networks

ments to oppose the construction of a wireless tower in their community. Instead the local governments are limited to regulation based on community planning standards, which manifest themselves in the form of visual control. The growth of camouflage tower industry has grown out of the fact that the only tool available to communities who oppose cell phone towers is to attempt to render them invisible. The ubiquitous cell tower camouflaged as a palm tree is an appropriate model for this private network building—an influence whose very power is hidden from the public's view.

Stealthy networks of towers and transmission stations span the city in a hexagonal matrix—combing a sprawling metropolis already shaped by generations of commercial development.[9] The wireless phone network has been built in stages: the first network provides thin coverage zones that produce revenue to finance perpetual growth over successive phases. Because of the piecemeal construction of cellular systems and relative low cost per transmission location, the cellular industry has lent itself to a type of financing much different than the heavy construction of power lines, freeways or aqueducts.[10] These earlier projects necessitated a large up front investment and long-term construction schedules, making them virtual monopolies by their nature. But as insubstantial and nimble systems that can be built out in stages and paid for by their own growth, such as wireless phone networks, have transformed the rules of urban development. This new paradigm has impacts beyond its own development, influencing other forms of public infrastructure to seek out privatization.

Today the private sector has assumed a leading role in energy production, education, prisons, and road systems, all of which seek to move towards a new concept of adaptability and efficiency modeled on the open market using the new forms of communication and technology to monitor peak demands and cost models. The wireless communication networks are paving a path for future development based on urban buying habits rather than public discourse.

The move from government-backed infrastructure to private networks has shifted power to such a degree that city governments are left to compete with each other to attract the latest technological boons, offering tax incentives and public lands for use by private entities in exchange for access to the latest gadgetry.

As concept, privatization appears an efficient and sound strategy for extending the reach and depth of the new urban infrastructure, and doing so without further taxing citizenry. However, we begin to understand the impacts of this business model only when we examine the implications of technology meeting the landscape. Examining the wireless coverage maps of Los Angeles exposes a definable hierarchy following the dense corridors through a city where the consumer roams, while neglecting neighborhoods with less viable demographics. Consumer polling, interest group research, and statistical usage data are tapped to understand the needs of the cellular citizens, at the expense of the collective needs of the community. Inevitable byproducts of this hierarchical development, dead zones emerge, areas not economical to build out as part of the network. The reality that parts of the city remain victims of "Swiss cheese" coverage becomes a concern to the networks only when the density of lost calls and complaints in a particular area triggers a corporate response. Although the operations of a smooth corporate hierarchy

are unquestionably more efficient, universal access is too expensive to be an immediate goal and in the end the corporation answers to the needs of the citizens only through many filters: stockholders, marketing images, cost-benefit ratios, and the bottom line.

Wireless nodes represent a dispersed network which typifies the city at both the macro and the micro-level. The integration of the wireless network into the daily workings of the city is particularly evident in the creative industries where film and television crews come together for short durations. In this model teams of experts form for a creative production which can last from a single day for a commercial, up to several months for a film, before dispersing again. Within this culture a wireless connection has become a necessity for instant communication with other workers about job leads and changing opportunities. This "Network Economy", as Manuel Castells has explained, "Represents a new form of entrepreneurship in which the individual worker markets his or her human capital portfolio among various 'buyers.'" [11] The culture of the network permeates the everyday life of the city, often times blurring the boundaries between work and leisure. Spaces like libraries, cafes, coffee shops and have become where business is transacted, not just among the heavy brokers, but also on all levels of the network culture.

The growth of wireless usage from being a luxury a decade ago, to a necessity today demonstrates the importance now placed on instant communications. In the Los Angeles wireless region alone (Los Angeles, Orange and Riverside counties), network users have doubled over the last 5 years; today there are over 14.6 million subscribers to the network, in a population of 18 million. [12] We are seeing the influence of this shift beyond the middle class, into the growing economy of freelance and gray markets jobs. Wireless technology is now a common tool for day laborers, landscapers, maintenance workers, mobile food vendors, and other "migratory" workers who each must keep in constant touch with clients and colleagues to negotiate for and locate work. With communication freed from the confines of land-based systems and adapted to the peripatetic body (mobile phones, smartphones, laptops) such individuals are able to leap beyond previous spatial barriers to create his or her own connections.

Hidden in the fabric of the city are the informal networks that sustain an economy. As Paul Virilio has observed, "we may have reached a point in the development of the city where the individual has supplanted physical territory as the dominant form of urban identity.[13] The wireless infrastructure heightens the mobility of the individual, transforming our notion of the city; it is no longer easy to decipher where Los Angeles begins or ends. The boundaries of the city blur, as the interactions that used to happen in face-to-face transactions have now been transplanted by distance-shrinking telephone conversations, e-mail and network connections.

Caller Identification

With the personal freedom afforded by a mobile system individuals must give up something: they must become completely transparent with the system. The cell phone user is always connected and always locatable, a byproduct of a 2005 directive from the Federal Communication Commission which mandated that all all cell phone carriers provide the ability to trace cell phone calls to a location within 100 meters or less. This requirement was neccesitated because of the increasing number of users opting out of land based phones, rendering the 911 emergency phone system with address tracking obsolete. To comply, the US wireless industry integrated GPS receivers into all their phones, so that even when not in use

the carriers can track its customers to within approximately 5 meters. Perversely, although the mobile phone user is always connected and always locatable within the network, the GPS system is rarely made available to handset owners, as their location data is collected behind the scenes. This data has become a useful feedback method for the cell phone companies to use their customers habits and location patterns in the planning and optimization of their networks.

When a cell phone call begins, a signal is sent to the nearest tower, which verifies the user's name and authorization and billing information. Once the caller is approved the tower connects like a normal call, but as the caller begins to move out of range of the first tower a signal is sent out, allowing the call to be handed off to the next tower. What appears to be one phone call is actually composed of many relays over different towers, as the network constantly tracks the caller in space. The information is then cataloged in digital form, open not only to data mining to expose possible new markets or for identifying areas of call density, but also can be exploited in the name of "security". This fundamental subservience inherent to a communication system was expressed by Jean Baudrillard: "The essential thing is to maintain a relational décor, where all the terms must continually communicate among themselves and stay in contact, informed of the respective condition of others and of the system as a whole, where opacity, resistance or the secrecy of a single term can lead to catastrophe."[14] So, with this freedom the individual must become completely transparent to allow the system to work. In this open market the individual is increasingly susceptible to the power of mass advertising that controls the trajectory of urban capital, deftly manipulating cultural trends.

Niche Markets

The urban citizen is vulnerable to the demographic mining

that both empowers and controls the daily lives of its citizens/customers. NexTel distinguished itself early, finding its niche with both building contractors and the predominantly Mexican-immigrant labor force. Developed to take advantage of the 2-way radio communication that had already been established in practice on construction jobs, push-to-talk technology was easily adopted for the communication needs of both management and construction workers on site. But NexTel's advantage had far deeper implications. Though one can only sell a limited number of phones to workers in the building trades, when accounting for other members of a construction worker's family and social group, the target of customers grows exponentially. A laborer, being the primary wage-earner, might be the first in his family or social group to purchase a phone, and will do so as a necessary expense of his employment. But when subsequent members move into a social or economic position to also subscribe for phone ser-vice, though push-to-talk may not be a required feature for their use, they will none-the-less be more familiar with NexTel via product exposure. Furthermore, if a NexTel subscriber is among the primary telephone contacts, they will be more likely to remain in the same network, taking advantage of free mobile-to-mobile service, in addition to push-to-talk ability.

NexTel may have taken an early lead among Latinos, but more telling still are their attempts to maintain this lead. Marketing has relied on traditional schemes, such as underwriting con-certs for Latino music, but so too has it undertaken strategies even more intricately tied to its customer-base. While American companies are politically limited to the nation of their operation—agreements with a Mexican firm in which the company holds a partial stake do exist—the signal has the ability to cross boundaries unfettered. In the early 21st century, without explicitly claiming an ability to use NexTel from the border regions of Baja California, billboards made reference

to the possibility that portions of northern Mexico were suddenly 'in network.' As federal policy increasingly solidified the boundary of the United States against illegal Mexican immigration, an American corporation was dematerializing the very same border to increase its appeal to a particular population that lived on both sides of that line.

Implications for Urban Development

Freeways, telephone, satellite networks and Wi-Fi networks, radio and television frequencies each provide means by which the everyday city flows and composes itself. This new open-ended Infrastructure doesn't dictate its form in concrete, but still has an immense impact on the life and consciousness of the city. While privately operated wireless infrastructure has had positive implications for individual freedom, allowing new opportunities for citizens to form their own connections to their surrounding community, it also exposes a troubling sovereignty now afforded corporations in the planning of American cities. A model of privatized infrastructure is be-coming increasingly prevalent, as civil institutions are declared obsolete. The privatization of governance through private police forces and prisons, private school districts and toll roads, all lead us towards a city further divided along economic lines and lacking a cohesive means of ensuring equal access. Under this private mantle urban development decisions more closely match the exchanges used in business: market share and price point find their relationship not with the public, but with other, competing infrastructures. Amortization of costs becomes part of the thought process, and those who do not fit a prescribed buying demographic are suddenly no longer part of the equation.

There is an unquestionable faith today in the ability of the market to respond to our needs, which makes the activities of government seem almost irrelevant in comparison. However,

as Gerald Frug has noted, there is a measurable difference
between how a consumer acts individually (seeking the cheapest
price for the largest return) versus how they will act when
voting on government measures that can benefit the many.[15]
The individual will often put the needs of society and the less
fortunate ahead of his own when casting a vote for a thing
like school bonds or street maintenance. The citizen/shopper
in a market system, by contrast, will only look out for his
pocketbook interests, at the expense of a larger urban vision.

The mega-city, fragmented and dispersed, must come to grips
with the new reality of mobile and malleable infrastructures,
and it must begin to compete with the private networks.
For the benefit of the citizenry, if we are to continue the development of a privatized infrastructure, we must find ways
of reactivating former operative logics, such as "the greater
good," with the new, economic privatized ecomomic regime.
Like the cellular networks themselves, today's cities must
form connections beyond their distinct geographic boundaries,
carving new systems of interaction and collective space on
a regional scale. Only in a borderless, regionally scaled city
plan organized by purpose rather than geographical
boundaries, can the public realm hope to compete with
the smooth surfaces of corporate control.

REFERENCES:

– Banham, Reyner. *Los Angeles, The Architecture of Four Ecologies.* Penguin Books, 1971.

– Baudrillard, Jean. "Ecstasy of Communications." From *The Anti-Esthetic*, edited by Hal Foster, trans. John Johnston. Seattle: Bay Press, 1983.

– Brodsly, David. *LA Freeway.* University of California Press, 1981.

– Castells, Manuel; Benner, Chris. "Labour markets and employment practices in the age of flexibility: a case study of Silicon Valley." *International Labour Review* v136, n1. Spring, 1997.

– Castells, Manuel. The Rise od Network Society. Blackwell publishers, 1996.

– DeLanda, Manuel. *Thousand Years of Non Linear History* Zone Books, 1998.

– Federal Communication Commission. 2006., "Annual Report and Analysis of Competitive Market Conditions with Respect to Commercial Mobile Services." *FCC Report* 06-142, 2006.

– Frug, Gerald E. *City Making.* Princeton University Press, 1999.

– Frug, Gerald E. "The City as Legal Concept." *Harvard Law Review, 1980.*

– Fulton, William. *The reluctant Metropolis: The Politics of Urban Growth in Los Angeles.* Solano Press Books, 1997.

– Graham, Stephan and Simon Marvin. *Splintering Urbanism.* Routledge, 2001.

– Pope, Albert. *Ladders.* Princeton Architectural Press, 1996.

– Virilio, Paul and Sylvere Lotringer. *Pure War*, Semiotext(e), 1983.

NOTES:

[1] See Albert pope's book Ladders.

[2] For example throughout the city still stand WWII-era air-raid sirens, typically a beige color, standing atop steel posts. This earlier system of telecommunications is rarely ever noted, as it too has faded into the visual clutter.

[3] As William Fulton explains in *The Reluctant Metropolis*, the growth machine that characterized Los Angeles for much of the last century was largely driven by real estate development, which in turn was dependent on a strong infrastructure of water and electricity to subsides the continuous expansion of the city through developments on the periphery. (Fulton 1997).

[4] As Fulton has explored, many of the civic and government officials of los angeles have been inextricably linked to land development for much of the past century. (Fulton 1997). Today the regional urban population as estimated by the census bureau for the combined statistical area for greater los Angeles is 12.9 million inhabitants.

[5] See Albert Pope's book *Ladders* for an extensive look at American cities and their transformation from places formed on the equal access of the gird to a closed system of the cul-de-sac or ladder.

[5] See Reyner Banham's book *Los Angeles, The Architecture of Four Ecologies*.

[6] In his work Gerald Frug traces the powerlessness of today's cites and the subsequent rise in Public Corporate powers, to our legal system and its favoring of individual rights over state rights. This historical power shift from public corpora-tions to private corporations is a product of our current legal systems propensity to ensure that Private Corporations are protected from state domination, while Public Corporations are subject to such domination.

[8] Quoted from Section 332(c)(7) of the Communications Act.

[9] The hexagonal grid is often referred to in the technical writing surrounding radio-based technology because it re-presents an ideal efficiency. The hexagon's symmetry means the distance between a given cell and its immediate neigh-bors is the same along any of the six main directions, thus it contains 12-fold symmetry as opposed to the rectangle's 8-fold symmetry.

[10] cost per transmission towers has been estimated at around $150,000 each by industry estimates.

[11] See Manuel Castells (1996).

[12] According to the FCC Southern California district potential customer base.

[13] See PaulVirilio's book *Pure War*.

[14] See Jean Baudrillard's essay *Ecstacy of Communications*, a prophetic text on the logic of communications systems.

[15] See Gerald Frug's Book *City Making* for a look at this concept of personal gain vs. greater good and its loss in most dis-cussion of privatization of public services.

TED KANE

TACO TRU

EMERGEI

③

U

"The evolution of a species is inseperable from the evolution of the environment. The two processes are tightly coupled as a single indivisible process" –JAMES LOVELOCK

IN LOS

Everyday in Los Angeles fleets of over 4000 mobile restaurants migrate through the streets in search of business.[1] The trucks respond to the daily changes of the city and its customers, piggybacking on the larger infrastructure of freeways, power, telephone and water systems to find a market for their services. The Taco Truck, or what the health department terms a Mobile Food Preparation Unit (MFPU)[2], follows its own path among an infinite number of potential routes through the city, yet the trucks' patterns of collective behavior reveal active responses to elements in the city. The truck is a fluid and mobile infrastructure overlaid onto existing roadways; as a mobile and adaptable system, the Taco Truck network provides a useful tool for exploring the underlying dynamics of a city –revealing spaces that would be impossible to discover using static models and conventional mapping tools.

Mobile Patterns

The typical day for a Taco Truck business begins before 5am in one of over 30 commissaries regulated by Los Angeles County.[3] At the commissaries the Taco Truck owner pays an average of $25 a day for a parking space, hot and cold water hookups, drains for cleaning the trucks, as well as access to a wholesale market for food, drinks, ice and propane. These commissaries are spread across the region, creating a dispersed network of centers from which a steady flow of restaurants span outward along independent routes. After preparing the truck and supplies a truck will typically head out by 6am. Each Taco Truck starts on equal footing, serving a potential market of 10 million residents.[4]

The extraordinary competition among the trucks guarantees that they are drawn to areas of demand. Because of their adaptive nature their appearance is an indication of a certain type of condition in the city that might not otherwise be visible. From the infinite potential paths patterns of clustering unexpectedly emerge, resulting from the unique overlay of particular geographic, social and economical conditions that together create an ideal breeding ground for a Taco Truck. For example the appearance of a Taco Truck in the wealthy neighborhoods of Beverly Hills or Malibu might seem unexpected, and yet they are tapping into a market of gardeners, nannies and day laborers who are isolated from affordable food. Following a Taco Truck for a day, such spaces of transient density suddenly become apparent, including the late night streets of Hollywood Boulevard, where prostitutes congregate; the city parks during soccer matches; day-labor pick-up and construction sites; downtown factories, ware-houses, film and TV location shoots; and the beachfront streets where surfers and sunbathers gather. Mobile restaurants are naturally drawn to these spaces of temporary density located on the periphery of established commercial districts, in areas that benefit from the cheap food and convenience of a curbside restaurant. Taco Trucks reconfigure these transient spaces into ad-hoc restaurant zones whenever and wherever the situation warrants.

Urban Connections

Communication is critical to the success of a Taco Truck, as a route is compiled from connections developed with factory foreman, construction contractors, and business owners, culled over many years. In this effort the cell phone has become a driver's indispensable tool, allowing for feedback from customers and adaption to different client schedules. The most lucrative routes for a mobile restaurant are at the factories around downtown LA where each 20-minute stop can serve several dozen clients. The Taco Truck owner will work closely with the site supervisors to time his stops with breakfast, lunch and coffee breaks, and through such service the drivers are able to inspire loyalty from clients and establish referrals to other similar sites.

The success of a Taco Truck business is closely related to an owner's ability to establish social and geographic connections to the city. Knowledge of the city and the areas of density is one of the things that distinguish an experienced driver from a beginner. A new driver must start by establishing a route through the city that will bring steady business, but this process is made more difficult by the unwritten code among drivers which impedes them from encroaching on another truck's territory unless specifically invited by a customer. This seniority system requires a new driver to span out farther beyond the established routes to find business. To accomplish this he will need to work the periphery of established sites in hope of finding underserved areas, or he may chose to work off hours when most of the trucks have finished their routes. It is common in the business for a beginning driver to start by taking on the route of an experienced driver with an established client base. The established driver will then expand his business by purchasing a second truck, thus becoming both a driver and manager of two routes and through this process eventually accumulating a fleet of several food vans.[5] Innovation comes with the introduction of new drivers; their constant searching uncovers previously undiscovered pockets of demand, creating complex niche markets and co-operatives that evolve through the constantly changing local conditions.

Cultural Symbols

The popularity of the Taco Truck is symbolic of a cultural shift visible in the growth of Latino residents in Los Angeles, where Latinos now makeup 47% of the population.[6] The immigrant population has created a fertile market of customers seeking the familiar foods from their homes at affordable prices; the common use of Spanish at the mobile restaurant also removes the language barrier that might otherwise make eating out less likely for new immigrants.[7] The connection of the Taco Truck or the "Lonchera" to the immigrant community has trig-gered cultural battles among communities insecure about an influx of unfamiliar food and culture. In New Orleans, where a large population of immigrant construction labor relocated following hurricane Katrina was soon followed by a boom in Taco Trucks. New Orleans recently passed laws to outlaw taco trucks exposing an anti-immigrant sentiment that manifested itself as a fear that Taco Trucks are unhealthy or would result in a loss of indigenous culture.[8] Such cultural food wars have popped up in other California cities including Salinas and San Bernardino, where Taco Trucks have also been banned from city streets. The health issue is often the reason cited for a city to ban Taco Trucks, even when the trucks are in compliance with health codes, as occurred in New Orleans – evidence of the power this cultural symbol has in exposing underlying tensions.[9]

The Taco Truck is predominately a small business enterprise with the owner also acting as driver. Taco Trucks work from the bottom up in forming a client base, and this personal connection to their clients may explain the passion many Angelinos feel toward particular trucks.[10] Through the development of a loyal clientele over time, an experienced Taco Truck will often graduate into a semi-permanent facility located in one or two locations for extended periods of the day. This change happens when the truck finds a location niche that can be exploited without the need for constant roaming, or when it develops a co-operative agreement with a business to use its parking lot as a basis of operations. The truck owner's goal is to find a location that has a density of clientele to sustain it for an extended period of the day, as this setup saves gas and establishes a repeat customer base who knows where to find the truck. While the transient Taco Truck moves quickly among lower-density locations to serve a diverse mix of needs, the semi-permanent truck takes on the location memory of a fixed restaurant. Many of

CKS:
T
RBANISM
ANGELES

these semi-permanent restaurants also take on the look of fixed restaurants with outdoor seating and the capacity for customers to call in orders, for pick up. A notable example of this type of food van is the La Isla Bonita seafood van that has been parking in the same spot on a Venice street from 6am-5pm for over a decade tapping into the needs of a regular crowd of construction workers, gardeners, beach goers, gym rats and film industry workers. On Alameda Blvd in downtown LA another semi-permanent Taco Truck regularly occupies the corner of an industrial parking lot where it caters to a steady flow of truck drivers, garment workers and security personnel.

Sedentary Trucks

In 2006 lobbying efforts by fixed site business with grievances about lost parking due to Taco Trucks persuaded the Los Angeles City Council to pass a law limiting to one hour the time that a Taco Truck can park in a commercial area, after which the truck must be moved more than a half-mile away for at least an hour before it can return to its original location.[11] Although irregularly inforced, this law has increased the occurrence of Taco Trucks leasing a parking spot in a commercial business lots during off business hours which allows them to park for extended periods without moving. This arrangement benefits both the truck, providing a fixed presence and saving money on gas, as well as the commercial business, providing extra income during off business hours. Such an arrangement is most common on busy arterial roads like Venice Blvd or Western Ave, where there is enough drive-by traffic to bring a steady flow of customers, compensating for the extra expense of a leased space.

The popularity of Taco Trucks and the advantage their flexibility brings has influenced several permanent restaurants to abandon their fixed location in favor of mobile restaurants, as their neighborhoods change or business wanes.[12] It is also common for fixed taco stands to simultaneously operate Taco Trucks in their parking lots. One such taco restaurant on Hoover avenue has a Taco Truck parked in its lot near the street to act as advertising; ironically the truck often has a line, while the fixed restaurant is empty. Some explanations for this might be the value associated with mobility, including the cheap price structure and speed of service implied by a truck, which makes the mobile restaurant more attractive to a potential customer.

Mobile Urban Models

In biological terms the Taco Truck could be considered an adaptive system where adaptation is the process by which an organism fits itself to its environment.[13] Only a few rules govern the behavior of Taco Trucks including the financial pressures of fuel prices, the social pressures of territoriality and the governmental pressures of traffic/parking and health laws. It is out of these frictions and customer demands that patterns develop in the physical reality of the city. The Taco Truck's adaptation to its physical environment exposes a pattern we can interpret and document through observation, providing a useful tool for seeing the transformation of urban space through time. However, we cannot map this system as a fixed entity, because its just one part of an infinite number of pathways and interrelated networks that make up the city. Los Angeles is a system co-evolving with it population, and cant be understood as a fixed entity, each moment the city reinventing itself, as are its inhabitants. Through the exploration of the impermanence inherent to the Taco Truck and other temporal forces, spaces of the city can be read and understood through their situational relationship rather than their fixed form. In this way the city can be better understood as a collection of interactions, which combine to create spaces of community, and it is through the exploration of these interactions that governments and planners can hope to provide a qualitative influence by fostering the emergence of positive relationships in the city. We can gain valuable insight about our culture by picking up the wheel behind a Taco Truck and discovering another way of mapping the city through the forces of economy, regulation, and politics, that a driver of a Taco Truck discovers inherently.[14]

REFERENCES:

– Baudrillard, Jean. *America*. Verso Press, 1988.

– Bustillo, Miguel. "Hold the tacos, New Orleans says." *Los Angeles Times*, July 14, 2007.

– Castells, Manuel. *The Rise of Network Society*. Blackwell Publishers, 1996.

– Holland, John H. *Hidden Order: How adaptation builds complexity*. Perseus Books Group, 1995.

– Katz, Jesse. "Wheels of Fortune." *Los Angeles Magazine*, October 2006.

– Kelly, Kevin. *Out of Control: The new biology of Machines, Social Systems, and the Economic World*. Perseus Books Group, 1994.

– Soja, Edward. *Postmetropolis: Critical Studies of Cities and Regions*. Blackwell Publishers, 2000.

NOTES:

[1] According to the Los Angeles County Department of Public Health Services there are around 2,400 registered and around 1,500 lapsed registered mobile restaurants (MFPU). It is estimated that there are several hundred unregistered vans operating illegally.

[2] MPFU is the term given to taco trucks by the State of California in their California Uniform Food Facilities Law (CURFFL) Article 12, which is enforced in Los Angeles by the LA County Dept of Health Services.

[3] All MFPU's must operate out of a commissary by state law. The commissaries are private business and are regulated by the LA County Department of Health Services.

[4] Based on the current US census for LA county.

[5] Los Angeles is the episcenter of Taco Truck fabrication with several factories. A fabricator on Slauson has been in business for over 25 years and brings in buyers from around the state and country. A new truck costs around $100,000 with financing available.

[6] See the Los Angeles County data sets published by the US Census Bureau. http://quickfacts.census.gov/qfd/states/06/06037.html

[7] From an interview with Luis Castro, the manager of Slauson foods commisary, he estimated that 80% of the workers have Spanish as their only language, but that most owners are bi-lingual. Personal interviews with drivers also confirmed this ratio.

[8] See LA Times article "Hold the tacos, New Orleans says" by Miguel Bustillo where he examines the growing Latino population in New Orleans that has quadrupled in the last 4 years while the overall population has decreased by half, causing tensions and fear among locals that new Orleans will lose its food history.

[9] The Los Angeles County Health Department by California Law

requires a yearly inspection, along with random inspections if there is a reason to suspect non-compliance. Since the trucks must be washed out nightly and leftover food disposed of, a regulated Taco Truck is most likely cleaner than fixed restaurants, this despite their reputation as roach coaches.

[10] When asked, nearly every Angelino seems to have a favorite taco truck restaurant to discuss. For some particularly passionate reviews of dozens of LA taco trucks see http://tacohunt.blogspot.com

[11] See LA City Ordinance 177620. available at http://cityclerk.lacity.org/CFI/DisplayOnlineDocument. cfm?SRT=D1&cfnum=05-2220
The amendment to the municipal code limits food vender parking in commercial areas for up to an hour, after which they must then move their trucks more than a half-mile away for at least an hour before they can return. In Residential neighborhoods this ordinance limits parking to 30 minutes.

[12] This occurred on several restaurants in Culver City where a taco stand was also operating a taco truck, eventually the stand closed leaving only the truck.

[13] See John Hollands' book *Hidden Order: How adaptation builds complexity* for a thorough examination of complex adaptive systems (cas).

[14] As Jean Baudrillard once wrote: "The point is not to write the sociology of the car, the point is to drive. That way you learn more about this society than all academia could ever tell you." Perhaps the point is also to drive a Taco Truck, and discover a city that might otherwise remain invisible to urban studies.

POLAR INERTIA BIBLIOGRAPHY:

- Appadurai, Arjun. *Modernity at Large: Cultural Dimensions of Globalization.* University of Minnesota Press, 1996.

- Banham, Reyner. *Los Angeles, The Architecture of Four Ecologies.* Penguin Books, 1971.

- Baudrillard, Jean. *America.* London: Verso Press, 1988.

- Baudrillard, Jean. "Ecstasy of Communications," from The Anti-Esthetic, edited by Hal Foster, trans. John Johnston. Bay Press, 1983.

- Brodsly, David. *LA Freeway.* University of California Press, 1981.

- Castells, Manuel. *The Rise of Network Society.* Massachusetts: Blackwell Publishers, 1996.

- Castells, Manuel; Benner, Chris. "Labour markets and employment practices in the age of flexibility: a case study of Silicon Valley." *International Labour Review v136, n1.* Spring, 1997.

- DeLanda, Manuel. *Thousand Years of Non Linear History.* Zone Books, 1998.

- Easterling, Keller, *Enduring Innocence: Global Architecture and Its Political Masquerades.* The MIT Press, 2005.

- Frug, Gerald E. *City Making.* Princeton University Press, 1999.

- Frug, Gerald E. "The City as Legal Concept". *Harvard Law Review, 1980.*

- Fulton, William. *The Reluctant Metropolis: The Politics of Urban Growth in Los Angeles.* Solano Press Books, 1997.

- Graham, Stephan and Simon Marvin. *Splintering Urbanism.* Routledge, 2001.

- Holland, John H. *Hidden Order: How adaptation builds complexity.* Perseus Books Group, 1995.

- Kelly, Kevin. *Out of Control: The new biology of Machines, Social Systems, and the Economic World.* Perseus Books, 1994.

- Pope, Albert. *Ladders.* Princeton Architectural Press, 1996.

- Soja, Edward. *Postmetropolis: Critical Studies of Cities and Regions.* Blackwell Publishers, 2000.

- Varnelis, Kazys and Sumrell, Robert. *Blue Monday: Stories of Absurd Realities and Natural Philosophies.* Actar Press, 2007.

- Virilio, Paul and Sylvere Lotringer. *Pure War,* Semiotext(e), 1983.

- Virilio, Paul. *Lost Dimension.* New York: Semiotext(e), 1991.

- Wallis Allan D. *Wheel Estate. The Rise and Decline of Mobile Homes.* The Johns Hopkins University Press, 1991.

ABOUT THE AUTHOR

Ted Kane is a photographer and architect living in California where he pursues urban research among the strip malls and car washes of greater Los Angeles. He completed his Bachelors in Architecture at the University of Kentucky and Masters in Architecture from the University of California, Los Angeles. In 2001, he founded the online journal **Polar Inertia** devoted to research on nomadic and popular culture, he continues to edit and publish six issues a year at **www.polarinertia.com**

ABOUT THE LOS ANGELES FORUM OF ARCHITECTURE AND URBAN DESIGN URBAN PAMPHLET SERIES

Moving quickly from concept to publication, the Forum Pamphlet series will focus on issues relating to the built environment of Southern California. The series will attempt to cover many diverse points of view, each reflecting on the vast geography of the region. Over time the series will aggregate to form a picture, however pixelated, of Los Angeles.

ACKNOWLEDGEMENTS

The completion of this project owes many thanks, foremost to the **LA Forum** and its board, particularly to its current and former directors **Michael Pinto**, **Kazys Varnelis**, **Warren Techentin**, who each led critical support. Thanks to **Tom Marble** for restarting the Pamphlet Series and for encouraging new reflections on the city. Thanks to **Greg Goldin** who read many early drafts and helped to elevate the readability factor and to **Penny Herscovitch** for her careful readings, edits and suggestions. Many informal conversations helped lead to the formulation of this material, and although there are too many to mention individually I would in particular like to thank **Matt Coolidge**, **Bryan Bell**, **Wes Janz**, **Kurt West**, and **Rick Miller** for their feedback. Thanks to Leo Huang for his tireless help during the printing process in Shanghai. Thanks also to my former professors **Keith Plymale**, **Mable Wilson** and **Jerzy Rozenberg** at the University of Kentucky and **Bob Somol**, **Ed Soja**, and **Thom Mayne** of UCLA who each influenced and contributed greatly to my way of seeing the world, even if they don't realize it. Thanks finally to Henri Lucas and Davey Whitcraft of **Willem Augustus** who's enthusiasm and talent have expertly presented this material and brought this publication to fruition.

a. **RV**s:

URBAN CAMPING

b. **RV**s:

BORDER CAMPING

c. CAMOUFLAGED

CELL PHONE TOWERS

d. LOS ANGELES

TACO TRUCKS

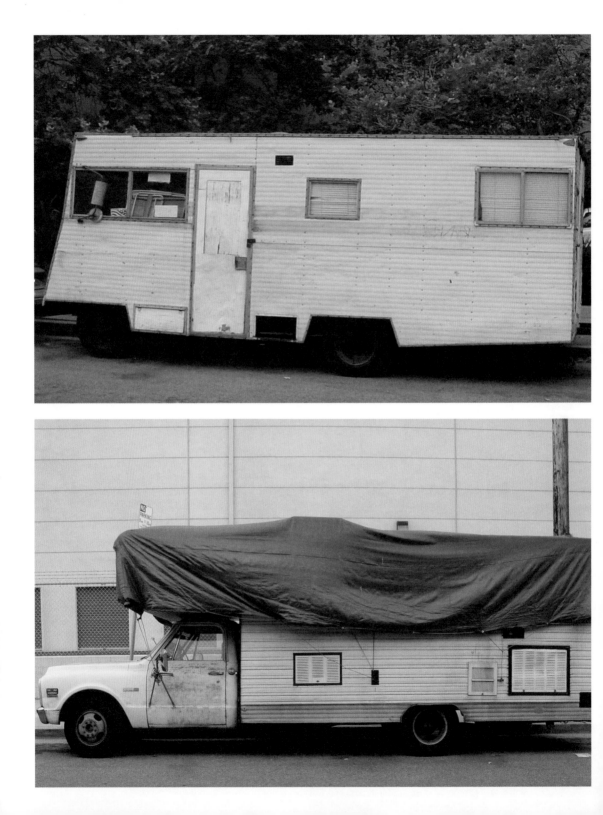

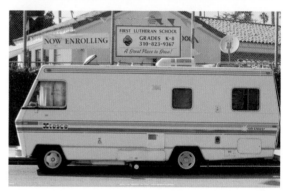